# British Warships & Auxiliaries

(1985/86 Edition)

£2.50

# THE ROYAL NAVY

After a 12 month period in which the Soviet Navy have increased their nuclear submarine fleet by nine, and five major units have joined the Surface Fleet—there can, unfortunately, be no reduction in the amount we, as a nation, spend to keep the Royal Navy as NATO's biggest—and best—European Navy.

Not only are these major warships appearing from Soviet shipyards at an impressive rate (they will soon be joined by a 65,000 ton aircraft carrier too) but the weapons fitted in these ships are being updated in an equally impressive way. Whilst CND rage about cruise missiles based in this country, it will not be long before the Soviets have a cruise missile at sea which can be launched from a submarine torpedo tube from many hundreds of miles away—or the Dover Straits. The missile (code named SS-NX-21) is not a naval tactical weapon but destined for attack against land targets. When the residents of our major cities realise the fact, it may take some of the steam out of the current campaign to remove the US weapons from our soil.

In the year that will see NATO celebrate 35 years of peace in Europe there will undoubtedly be much made of the fact. It is an achievement indeed, but it should not be forgotten that despite the increase in the number of ships in the US Navy, the build up of the Soviet fleet continues unabated. At present NATO commanders are warning that NATO has "a slender but decreasing edge over the Soviet navy . . . the overall figures of ships available to NATO are depressing and the trends are adverse."

Admirals, since time immemorial, have always demanded more ships—but they don't come cheap. With more and more pressure on the national budget for a share of the financial cake we can almost pat ourselves on the back for the amount we do spend on our navy. Let it not be forgotten however, that, as an island nation, we fail to do so at our peril . . . we also neglect the size and shape of our merchant marine at our peril too. Drastic action is currently needed in that area now. to halt its rapid decline.

During 1984 we have only seen four major warships join the Fleet—all packed with the latest technology of course, but the overall number of hulls in the Fleet is decreasing.

Fine ships are joining the Fleet, and old faithfuls are being refitted, but still there is no reduction in the Navy's worldwide commitments to compensate for the reduction in the number of its ships. It means of course that the current Fleet is being worked to the limit—with knock on effects to both machinery—and manpower.

The South Atlantic is still a major "drain" on Fleet units with ships on passage, repairing and preparing to go south taking a large proportion of the Fleet away from its NATO operating area. The so called, Gulf Patrol (ships are not allowed to enter the Gulf but are "on call" outside the area—often hundreds of miles away) and the requirement to provide a West Indies guardship do not leave many ships to fulfil commitments in home waters when ships in refit are deleted from the operators' lists of vessels available for the thousand and one jobs the modern navy is asked to fulfil.

It is very easy for "armchair admirals" to point out the Navy's warts—and that can be a good thing too—but let it be recorded that with the continuing arrival of more SSN's, Ark Royal and a handful of Type 24 and 22 ships, we are at least holding our own—and giving a strong lead to other NATO navies who could/should be doing more.

Many readers will sigh with relief that many of the decisions of the well remembered 1981 Defence Review are either being quietly forgotten—or reversed. The decision to place a group of Leander Class ships into the standby squadron has been reversed—and their retention in the Fleet can only be welcomed. These ships are undoubtedly "tired" now, having been worked very hard indeed in recent years. With the Reserve Fleet on the horizon, many of these ships had let the maintenance schedules slip and the dockyards have large work packages on them—to give them a few more years of useful life. Their retention in the Fleet can only be seen as a stop gap—replacement orders are necessary. Major refits are expensive but necessary—despite the title given to them—and the fact the politicians think a fleet can be worked hard and then given a lick of paint to keep it going. There does come a point however when ships become just too expensive to keep operational—and their equipment too ancient for a leading NATO sea-power. The not inconsiderable fleet of conventional submarines is rapidly becoming such a case. These boats, which have all served for 20-25 years, need replacing. The submarine branch have had the promises—now they need the boats . . .

The ability to refit our nuclear submarines has been a sore point in past years. The situation is being given top priority and now that many lessons have been learnt in the refitting of these capital ships, better turn round times being achieved by Devonport dockyard which has the commitment to refit the SSN Fleet. With the decision to refit the Trident submarines at Rosyth more submarine refit capacity is still needed if the ever increasing submarine fleet is to be kept operational. Capacity is also needed to repair running submarines—without penalty to the submarines under refit. Facilities are undoubtedly tight but the personnel involved are obviously dedicated to achieving the very tight deadlines demanded for these boats.

Major improvements are planned for the Devonport Yard and once the implications of the current dockyard reviews are announced the long term future of the yard is well assured—despite changes which may be made in its overall management.

The price however, to be paid to move work from Portsmouth to Rosyth may not be small. With large amounts of real estate at Portsmouth not fully used it seems questionable to move work—such as the refitting of the Type 42 destroyers to Rosyth. Office and accommodation space at Rosyth is limited—and special facilities are having to be built to accommodate both men and the ships themselves. Jetties are being extended to accommodate these ships—whilst jetties and facilities remain idle at Portsmouth. The cost of this move can also be expected to be felt by the personnel involved. A winter spent in the South Atlantic, followed by a winter refitting at Rosyth for a ships company of a Type 42—most of whom are Portsmouth based men—will undoubtedly take its toll of men wishing to leave the Navy for a second career in industry. The divorce rate amongst men in these ships could also be a sad reflection on this decision to move north. Time, and the ability of other yards to cope, could see a move of more work back to Portsmouth—and it is not beyond the realms of possibility to see commercial contractors refitting ships at Portsmouth using Ministry facilities.

The last year of speculation has given the dockyards the jolt they need—when jobs are at stake it concentrates the minds of the workers. There seems to be a new, realistic, attitude in the yards—the men seem determined to compete with commercial ship repairers. To do so, it is clear manpower will have to be trimmed but given the will to succeed the future could be bright. The "comparison refits" of two frigates and submarines in commercial yards will be watched with great interest—if only to see how much the supervision of the exercise costs—but the major decisions on the way ahead for the yards will have to be made long before the results of the comparisons are complete.

The closure of the Gibraltar dockyard will not be noticed in any significant way but the situation can be envisaged of the new commercial yard not having the capacity to repair NATO warships in the coming years at this the vital "choke point" of the Mediterranean/Atlantic. The yard's commercial position looks good under civilian management—but the Navy can not expect to be a priority customer.

The arguments regarding the Trident project will doubtless rumble on—and may even outlast the long running Conqueror/ Belgrano debate—which doubtless leaves the thinking reader utterly bored.

Trident is probably a necessity of the nineties but the costs, even at this early stage, are enormous. There can be little doubt that the naval budget and the coventional fleet of the future will reflect the decision to proceed.

With the constant aim to provide balanced fleet much could be done to improve the number of ships in the Fleet if Trident money was available to spend on conventional forces—and in this country.

A new class of frigate and a possible "downmarket" patrol vessel could be ships that are built in smaller numbers to help finance Trident. There are many roles a nuclear submarine—let alone Tirdent—cannot fulfil and the requirement for surface ships remain as vital today as they have ever been.

It will be interesting to see if the changes in the corridors of power at the Ministry of Defence have any noticeable effect on the hardware the Fleet is given or the way the Navy is run.

Manpower has been a problem over the recent years of change and uncertainty. To get the recruiting targets right must cause a few headaches for the long term planners. Officer recruiting is reasonable—apart from the constant problem of recruiting Observers (surely a name change to reflect the tactical skills of these aviators would help) plus engineer and instructor officers. Larger numbers of officers are now required and to get the message home to a school population who think the Navy is still cutting and cutting is an uphill task.

Rating recruitment is generally good—except in the area of the artificer apprentice. Industry gives the Navy a constant challenge to recruit the best potential technicians the schools can produce. For the girls trying to get into the WRENS or QARNNS however the story is very different—places are few and the competition for them is intense.

One of the major decisions that will have to be taken in the near future is that of the replacement for the assault ships FEARLESS and INTREPID—and to fill the gap left by the retirement of HERMES from the active fleet. The Royal Marines will shortly be desperate for dedicated "lift and shift" capacity to get them to their operating areas in Norway—or elsewhere should the need arise. Stop gap measures using merchant ships have only been partially successful. Mexifloats and helicopter pads are not found on conventional merchant ships and they have been badly needed in recent exercises. The Ministry's experience in purchasing redundant merchant ships for service under the white (and blue) ensign has not been good. Going for the cheapest tender has not proved good economics.

If the merchant service find a vessels uneconomic to operate it is a fair bet the vessel is "well used". The merchant service do not maintain their vessels to the same standard as the RN—and some very dubious purchases have been made in recent years. One hopes that the assault ship replacements at least will bring new orders to our work-starved shipyards rather than the MoD accept a cheap (in the short term) compromise.

"Value for money" will doubtless be the watchword for the late eighties. Undoubtedly there are still some areas where huge savings can still be made—but it is the corner cutting at the coal face that needs to be pondered over long and hard by the politicians. One trusts they accept the advice that is given them by their naval advisors who have the experience necessary to give this country the best defence our pockets can afford.

---

## SHIPS OF THE ROYAL NAVY — PENNANT NUMBERS

| Ship | Penn. No. | Ship | Penn. No. |
|---|---|---|---|
| **Aircraft Carriers** | | ANDROMEDA | F57 |
| INVINCIBLE | R05 | HERMIONE | F58 |
| ILLUSTRIOUS | R06 | JUPITER | F60 |
| ARK ROYAL | R09 | APOLLO | F70 |
| HERMES | R12 | SCYLLA | F71 |
| **Destroyers** | | ARIADNE | F72 |
| GLAMORGAN | D19 | CHARYBDIS | F75 |
| FIFE | D20 | BROADSWORD | F88 |
| BRISTOL | D23 | BATTLEAXE | F89 |
| BIRMINGHAM | D86 | BRILLIANT | F90 |
| NEWCASTLE | D87 | BRAZEN | F91 |
| GLASGOW | D88 | BOXER | F92 |
| EXETER | D89 | BEAVER | F93 |
| SOUTHAMPTON | D90 | BRAVE | F94 |
| NOTTINGHAM | D91 | LONDON | F95 |
| LIVERPOOL | D92 | SHEFFIELD | F96 |
| MANCHESTER | D95 | YARMOUTH | F101 |
| GLOUCESTER | D96 | LOWESTOFT | F103 |
| EDINBURGH | D97 | ROTHESAY | F107 |
| YORK | D98 | LEANDER | F109 |
| CARDIFF | D108 | FALMOUTH | F113 |
| **Frigates** | | AJAX | F114 |
| AURORA | F10 | BERWICK | F115 |
| ACHILLES | F12 | PLYMOUTH | F126 |
| EURYALUS | F15 | PENELOPE | F127 |
| DIOMEDE | F16 | AMAZON | F169 |
| GALATEA | F18 | ACTIVE | F171 |
| CLEOPATRA | F28 | AMBUSCADE | F172 |
| ARETHUSA | F38 | ARROW | F173 |
| NAIAD | F39 | ALACRITY | F174 |
| SIRIUS | F40 | AVENGER | F185 |
| PHOEBE | F42 | **Submarines** | |
| TORQUAY | F43 | SEALION | S07 |
| MINERVA | F45 | WALRUS | S08 |
| DANAE | F47 | OBERON | S09 |
| JUNO | F52 | ODIN | S10 |
| ARGONAUT | F56 | ORPHEUS | S11 |

| Ship | Penn. No. | Ship | Penn. No. |
|---|---|---|---|
| OLYMPUS | S12 | CATTISTOCK | M31 |
| OSIRIS | S13 | COTTESMORE | M32 |
| ONSLAUGHT | S14 | BROCKLESBY | M33 |
| OTTER | S15 | MIDDLETON | M34 |
| ORACLE | S16 | DULVERTON | M35 |
| OCELOT | S17 | ATHERSTONE | M36 |
| OTUS | S18 | CHIDDINGFOLD | M37 |
| OPOSSUM | S19 | BICESTER | M38 |
| OPPORTUNE | S20 | HURWORTH | M39 |
| ONYX | S21 | ALFRISTON | M1103 |
| RESOLUTION | S22 | BICKINGTON | M1109 |
| REPULSE | S23 | BILDESTON | M1110 |
| RENOWN | S26 | BRERETON | M1113 |
| REVENGE | S27 | BRINTON | M1114 |
| UPHOLDER | S40 | BRONINGTON | M1115 |
| CHURCHILL | S46 | WILTON | M1116 |
| CONQUEROR | S48 | CRICHTON | M1124 |
| COURAGEOUS | S50 | CUXTON | M1125 |
| TRENCHANT | S91 | BOSSINGTON | M1133 |
| VALIANT | S102 | GAVINTON | M1140 |
| WARSPITE | S103 | HODGESTON | M1146 |
| SCEPTRE | S104 | HUBBERSTON | M1147 |
| SPARTAN | S105 | IVESTON | M1151 |
| SPLENDID | S106 | KEDLESTON | M1153 |
| TRAFALGAR | S107 | KELLINGTON | M1154 |
| SOVEREIGN | S108 | KIRKLISTON | M1157 |
| SUPERB | S109 | MAXTON | M1165 |
| TURBULENT | S110 | NURTON | M1166 |
| TIRELESS | S117 | POLLINGTON | M1173 |
| TORBAY | S118 | SHAVINGTON | M1180 |
| SWIFTSURE | S126 | SHERATON | M1181 |
| | | UPTON | M1187 |
| **Assault Ships** | | WALKERTON | M1188 |
| FEARLESS | L10 | WOTTON | M1195 |
| INTREPID | L11 | SOBERTON | M1200 |
| **Minesweepers** | | STUBBINGTON | M1204 |
| **& Minehunters** | | WAVENEY | M2003 |
| BRECON | M29 | CARRON | M2004 |
| LEDBURY | M30 | DOVEY | M2005 |

| Ship | Penn. No. | Ship | Penn. No. |
|---|---|---|---|
| HELFORD | M2006 | ORKNEY | P299 |
| HUMBER | M2007 | LINDISFARNE | P300 |
| BLACKWATER | M2008 | BEACHAMPTON | P1007 |
| ITCHEN | M2009 | MONKTON | P1055 |
| HELMSDALE | M2010 | WASPERTON | P1089 |
| ORWELL | M2011 | WOLVERTON | P1093 |
| RIBBLE | M2012 | YARNTON | P1096 |
| SPEY | M2013 | **Minelayer** | |
| ARUN | M2014 | ABDIEL | N21 |
| **Patrol Craft** | | **Survey Ships & RN Manned Auxiliaries** | |
| PEACOCK | P239 | | |
| PLOVER | P240 | BRITANNIA | A00 |
| STARLING | P241 | ECHO | A70 |
| SWALLOW | P242 | ENTERPRISE | A71 |
| SWIFT | P243 | EGERIA | A72 |
| PROTECTOR | P244 | GLEANER | A86 |
| GUARDIAN | P245 | MANLY | A92 |
| SENTINEL | P246 | MENTOR | A94 |
| ALERT | P252 | MILBROOK | A97 |
| VIGILANT | P254 | MESSINA | A107 |
| LEEDS CASTLE | P258 | HECLA | A133 |
| KINGFISHER | P260 | HECATE | A137 |
| CYGNET | P261 | HERALD | A138 |
| PETEREL | P262 | HYDRA | A144 |
| SANDPIPER | P263 | ENDURANCE | A171 |
| DUMBARTON | | WAKEFUL | A236 |
| CASTLE | P265 | ETTRICK | A274 |
| ANGLESEY | P277 | ELSING | A277 |
| ALDERNEY | P278 | IRONBRIDGE | A311 |
| ATTACKER | P281 | BULLDOG | A317 |
| CHASER | P282 | IXWORTH | A318 |
| FENCER | P283 | BEAGLE | A319 |
| HUNTER | P284 | FOX | A320 |
| STRIKER | P285 | FAWN | A335 |
| JERSEY | P295 | WATERWITCH | M2720 |
| GUERNSEY | P297 | WOODLARK | M2780 |
| SHETLAND | P298 | CHALLENGER | K07 |

HMS Renown

## RESOLUTION CLASS

| Ship | Pennant Number | Completion Date | Builder |
|---|---|---|---|
| RESOLUTION | S22 | 1967 | Vickers |
| REPULSE | S23 | 1968 | Vickers |
| RENOWN | S26 | 1968 | C. Laird |
| REVENGE | S27 | 1969 | C. Laird |

**Displacement** 8,400 tons (submerged) **Dimensions** 130m x 10m x 9m **Speed** 25 knots **Armament** 16 Polaris Missiles, 6 Torpedo Tubes **Complement** 147 (x 2).

**Notes**

These four nuclear-powered Polaris submarines are the United Kingdom's contribution to NATO's strategic nuclear deterrent. At least one of them is constantly on patrol and because of their high speed, long endurance underwater, and advanced sonar and electronic equipment they have little fear of detection.

Each submarine carries 16 Polaris two-stage ballistic missiles, powered by solid fuel rocket motors, 9.45 metres long, 1.37 metres diameter and weighing 12,700 kilogrammes. Fired from the submerged submarine it can devastate a target 2,500 nautical miles away.

HMS Conqueror

## VALIANT CLASS

| Ship | Pennant Number | Completion Date | Builder |
|---|---|---|---|
| CHURCHILL | S46 | 1970 | Vickers |
| CONQUEROR | S48 | 1971 | C. Laird |
| COURAGEOUS | S50 | 1971 | Vickers |
| VALIANT | S102 | 1966 | Vickers |
| WARSPITE | S103 | 1967 | Vickers |

**Displacement** 4,900 tons dived **Dimensions** 87m x 10m x 8m **Speed** 28 knots + **Armament** 6 Torpedo Tubes **Complement** 103.

**Notes**
DREADNOUGHT—the forerunner of this class—is now awaiting disposal (by scrap or sinking) at Rosyth. These boats are capable of high underwater speeds and can remain on patrol almost indefinitely. They are able to circumnavigate the world without surfacing.

HMS Swiftsure

## SWIFTSURE CLASS

| Ship | Pennant Number | Completion Date | Builder |
|---|---|---|---|
| SCEPTRE | S104 | 1978 | Vickers |
| SPARTAN | S105 | 1979 | Vickers |
| SPLENDID | S106 | 1980 | Vickers |
| SOVEREIGN | S108 | 1974 | Vickers |
| SUPERB | S109 | 1976 | Vickers |
| SWIFTSURE | S126 | 1973 | Vickers |

**Displacement** 4,500 tons dived **Dimensions** 83m x 10m x 8m **Speed** 30 knots + dived **Armament** 5 Torpedo Tubes **Complement** 116.

**Notes**
A follow-on class of ships from the successful Valiant Class. These submarines have an updated Sonar and Torpedo system and are the very latest in submarine design. A new class of updated Swiftsure Class are now joining the Fleet.

HMS Turbulent

## TRAFALGAR CLASS

| Ship | Pennant Number | Completion Date | Builder |
|---|---|---|---|
| TRENCHANT | S91 | | Vickers |
| TRAFALGAR | S107 | 1983 | Vickers |
| TURBULENT | S110 | 1984 | Vickers |
| TIRELESS | S117 | 1985 | Vickers |
| TORBAY | S118 | | Vickers |

**Displacement** 4,500 tons **Dimensions** 85m x 10m x 8m **Speed** 30+ dived **Armament** 5 Torpedo Tubes **Complement** 97.

**Notes**
Designed to be considerably quieter than previous submarines. Hull is covered with noise reducing tiles. These boats also have a greater endurance & speed than their predecessors.

HMS Walrus

## PORPOISE CLASS

| Ship | Pennant Number | Completion Date | Builder |
|---|---|---|---|
| SEALION | S07 | 1961 | C. Laird |
| WALRUS | S08 | 1961 | Scotts |

**Displacement** 2,410 tons (submerged) **Dimensions** 90m x 8m x 5m **Speed** 12 knots surfaced, 17 submerged **Armament** 8 Torpedo Tubes **Complement** 70.

**Notes**
Diesel powered submarines that were the first to be designed and built after the war. Capable of long under-water patrols, but mainly used for exercise and training purposes as more Nuclear submarines join the Fleet. The 1981 Defence review stated "We will proceed as fast as possible with a new and more effective class to replace our ageing diesel-powered submarines". By late 1984 a single order for one submarine (to be named UPHOLDER) had been placed— more are expected.

HMS Olympus

## OBERON CLASS

| Ship | Pennant Number | Completion Date | Builder |
|---|---|---|---|
| OBERON | S09 | 1961 | Chatham D'yard |
| ODIN | S10 | 1962 | C. Laird |
| ORPHEUS | S11 | 1960 | Vickers |
| OLYMPUS | S12 | 1962 | Vickers |
| OSIRIS | S13 | 1964 | Vickers |
| ONSLAUGHT | S14 | 1962 | Chatham D'yard |
| OTTER | S15 | 1962 | Scotts |
| ORACLE | S16 | 1963 | C. Laird |
| OCELOT | S17 | 1964 | Chatham D'yard |
| OTUS | S18 | 1963 | Scotts |
| OPOSSUM | S19 | 1964 | C. Laird |
| OPPORTUNE | S20 | 1964 | Scotts |
| ONYX | S21 | 1967 | C. Laird |

**Displacement** 2,410 tons (submerged) **Dimensions** 90m x 8m x 5m **Speed** 12 knots surface, 17 knots submerged **Armament** 8 Torpedo Tubes **Complement** 70.

**Notes**
OLYMPUS is fitted with a 5 man chamber to allow exit & re-entry of the submarine whilst dived—a facility used by Royal Marine special forces.

HMS Ark Royal

## INVINCIBLE CLASS

| Ship | Pennant Number | Completion Date | Builder |
|---|---|---|---|
| INVINCIBLE | R05 | 1979 | Vickers |
| ILLUSTRIOUS | R06 | 1982 | Swan-Hunter |
| ARK ROYAL | R09 | 1985 | Swan-Hunter |

**Displacement** 19,500 tons **Dimensions** 206m x 32m x 6.5m **Speed** 28 knots **Armament** Sea Dart Missile, 2 x 20mm guns, 2 Phalanx **Aircraft** 5 x Sea Harrier, 10 x Sea King **Complement** 900 + aircrews.

**Notes**
When ARK ROYAL is completed—two ships will be kept in the operational fleet at any one time—the other being in refit/ reserve.
ARK ROYAL's external appearance differs somewhat from the other two ships.

HMS Hermes

## HERMES CLASS

| Ship | Pennant Number | Completion Date | Builder |
|---|---|---|---|
| HERMES | R12 | 1959 | Vickers |

**Displacement** 28,700 tons **Dimensions** 229m x 27m x 9m **Speed** 28 knots **Armament** 2 Sea Cat Missile Systems, 9 Sea King helicopters, 5 Sea Harrier aircraft, 2 Wessex helicopters **Complement** 980 + aircrews.

**Notes**
A former fixed wing aircraft carrier converted to a Commando Carrier in 1971-73. Refitted in 1976 into an anti-submarine Carrier and again in 1981 (for Sea Harrier operations). Flagship for the Falkland Islands Task Force. In 1984, reduced to a harbour training ship at Portsmouth—officially at 30 days' notice for sea. A small ships company remains. A decision on her fate is expected in the summer of 1985.

HMS Fearless

## FEARLESS CLASS

| Ship | Pennant Number | Completion Date | Builder |
|---|---|---|---|
| FEARLESS | L10 | 1965 | Harland & Wolff |
| INTREPID | L11 | 1967 | J. Brown |

**Displacement** 12,500 tons, 19,500 tons(flooded) **Dimensions** 158m x 24m x 8m **Speed** 20 knots **Armament** 4 Sea Cat Missile Systems, 2·x 40mm guns **Complement** 580.

**Notes**
Multi-purpose ships that can operate helicopters for embarked Royal Marine Commandos. 4 landing craft are carried on an internal deck and are flooded out when ship docks down. One ship is usually in refit/reserve. The other is used to train young officers from the RN College, Dartmouth (currently FEARLESS), but still retains amphibious capabilities. INTREPID will replace FEARLESS during 1985 in the Dartmouth rôle.

HMS Bristol

**BRISTOL CLASS (Type 82)**

| Ship | Pennant Number | Completion Date | Builder |
|---|---|---|---|
| BRISTOL | D23 | 1972 | Swan Hunter |

**Displacement** 6,750 tons **Dimensions** 154m x 17m x 7m **Speed** 30 knots + **Armament** 1 x 4.5" gun, Ikara Anti-submarine Missile System, 1 Sea Dart Missile System, 2 x 20mm guns **Complement** 407.

**Notes**
Four ships of this class were ordered but three later cancelled when requirement for large escorts for fixed wing aircraft carriers ceased to exist. Helicopter Deck provided but no aircraft normally carried. Now used as a Flagship. Early retirement was planned but will now be retained in the active Fleet for at least a further five years. In refit throughout 1985 at Portsmouth.

HMS Glamorgan

## COUNTY CLASS

| Ship | Pennant Number | Completion Date | Builder |
|---|---|---|---|
| GLAMORGAN | D19 | 1966 | Vickers |
| FIFE | D20 | 1966 | Fairfield |

**Displacement** 6,200 tons **Dimensions** 159m x 16m x 6m **Speed** 32 knots **Armament** 2 x 4.5″ guns, 2 x 20mm guns, 4 x 30mm guns, 4 Exocet Missiles, 1 x Sea Slug Missile System. Seacat. Torpedo Tubes **Complement** 485.

**Notes**
A Lynx helicopter is now carried in lieu of the original Wessex Mk3. GLAMORGAN has 2 x 40mm guns. ANTRIM was sold to Chile in 1984. GLAMORGAN to be a training ship in 1985.

**HMS Liverpool**

## SHEFFIELD CLASS (Type 42)

| Ship | Pennant Number | Completion Date | Builder |
|---|---|---|---|
| BIRMINGHAM | D86 | 1976 | C. Laird |
| NEWCASTLE | D87 | 1978 | Swan Hunter |
| GLASGOW | D88 | 1978 | Swan Hunter |
| EXETER | D89 | 1980 | Swan Hunter |
| SOUTHAMPTON | D90 | 1981 | Vosper T. |
| NOTTINGHAM | D91 | 1982 | Vosper T. |
| LIVERPOOL | D92 | 1982 | C. Laird |
| ● MANCHESTER | D95 | 1983 | Vickers |
| ● GLOUCESTER | D96 | 1984 | Vosper T. |
| ● EDINBURGH | D97 | 1984 | C. Laird |
| ● YORK | D98 | 1984 | Swan Hunter |
| CARDIFF | D108 | 1979 | Vickers |

**Displacement** 3,660 tons **Dimensions** 125m x 15m x 7m **Speed** 30 knots + **Armament** 1 x 4.5″ gun, 4 x 30mm guns, 4 x 20mm guns, Sea Dart Missile System: Lynx Helicopter. 6 Torpedo Tubes **Complement** 280 + ● "stretched" Type 42.

**Notes**

● "Stretched" versions are 14 metres longer than earlier vessels of the class.

**HMS Boxer**

## BROADSWORD CLASS (Type 22)

| Ship | Pennant Number | Completion Date | Builder |
|---|---|---|---|
| BROADSWORD | F88 | 1978 | Yarrow |
| BATTLEAXE | F89 | 1980 | Yarrow |
| BRILLIANT | F90 | 1981 | Yarrow |
| BRAZEN | F91 | 1982 | Yarrow |
| ● BOXER | F92 | 1983 | Yarrow |
| ● BEAVER | F93 | 1984 | Yarrow |
| ● BRAVE | F94 | 1985/6 | Yarrow |
| ● LONDON | F95 | Building | Yarrow |
| SHEFFIELD | F96 | Building | Swan Hunter |
| COVENTRY | | Building | Swan Hunter |

**Displacement** 3,860 tons **Dimensions** 131m x 15m x 4m **Speed** 29 knots **Armament** 4 Exocet Missiles, 2 Sea Wolf Missile Systems, 2 x 40mm guns, 6 Torpedo Tubes, 2 Lynx Helicopters **Complement** 224/290 ● "Stretched" Type 22 (4,400 tons).

**Notes**
An order for a further two ships is expected. Later (Batch 3) ships will carry a 4.5" gun in lieu of the 40mm fitted in earlier ships and 8 surface-to-surface guided weapons in lieu of 4. They will be able to operate EH101 (Sea King replacement) helicopters.

HMS Ariadne

## LEANDER CLASS

| Ship | Pennant Number | Completion Date | Builder |
|---|---|---|---|
| ACHILLES | F12 | 1970 | Yarrow |
| DIOMEDE | F16 | 1971 | Yarrow |
| JUNO | F52 | 1967 | Thornycroft |
| APOLLO | F70 | 1972 | Yarrow |
| ARIADNE | F72 | 1972 | Yarrow |

**Displacement** 2,962 tons **Dimensions** 113m x 13m x 5m **Speed** 27 knots **Armament** 2 x 4.5″ guns, 3 x 20mm guns, 1 Sea Cat Missile system, 1 Mortar Mk10, 1 Wasp helicopter **Complement** 260.

**Notes**
JUNO will replace TORQUAY as a Training Ship during 1985. Most of these ships were destined for the Standby Squadron but will now remain in service—after refits to bring them up to modern standards.

HMS Leander

## LEANDER CLASS (Ikara Conversions)

| Ship | Pennant Number | Completion Date | Builder |
|---|---|---|---|
| AURORA | F10 | 1964 | J. Brown |
| EURYALUS | F15 | 1964 | Scotts |
| GALATEA | F18 | 1964 | S. Hunter |
| ARETHUSA | F38 | 1965 | Whites |
| NAIAD | F39 | 1965 | Yarrow |
| LEANDER | F109 | 1963 | Harland & Wolff |
| AJAX | F114 | 1963 | C. Laird |

**Displacement** 2,860 tons **Dimensions** 113m x 12m x 5m **Speed** 29 knots **Armament** 1 Ikara Anti-submarine Missile, 2 x 40mm guns, 2 Sea Cat Missile Systems, 1 Mortar Mk10, 1 Wasp helicopter **Complement** 240.

**Notes**

All ships were converted (1973-76) to carry the Ikara Anti-submarine Missile System (forward of the bridge) in lieu of a 4.5″ gun. The Wasp helicopter is being replaced in most ships by the Lynx. Earlier plans to reduce some ships to reserve will not now be implemented.

**HMS Andromeda**

## LEANDER CLASS (Sea Wolf Conversions)

| Ship | Pennant Number | Completion Date | Builder |
|---|---|---|---|
| ANDROMEDA | F57 | 1968 | HM Dockyard Portsmouth |
| HERMIONE | F58 | 1969 | Stephen |
| JUPITER | F60 | 1969 | Yarrow |
| SCYLLA | F71 | 1970 | HM Dockyard Devonport |
| CHARYBDIS | F75 | 1969 | Harland & Wolff |

**Displacement** 2,962 tons **Dimensions** 113m x 13m x 5m **Speed** 27 knots **Armament** Sea Wolf System, 4 x Exocet Missiles, 2 x 40mm guns, 1 Lynx helicopter **Complement** 260.

**Notes**
The refitting of these ships has cost in the region of £70m—ten times their original cost—but they are now packed with the latest anti-submarine technology.

HMS Phoebe

**LEANDER CLASS (Exocet Conversions)**

| Ship | Pennant Number | Completion Date | Builder |
|---|---|---|---|
| CLEOPATRA | F28 | 1966 | HM Dockyard Devonport |
| SIRIUS | F40 | 1966 | HM Dockyard Portsmouth |
| PHOEBE | F42 | 1966 | Stephens |
| MINERVA | F45 | 1966 | Vickers |
| DANAE | F47 | 1967 | HM Dockyard Devonport |
| ARGONAUT | F56 | 1967 | Hawthorn Leslie |
| PENELOPE | F127 | 1963 | Vickers |

**Displacement** 2,860 tons **Dimensions** 113m x 12m x 5m **Speed** 27 knots **Armament** 4 Exocet Missiles, 3 Sea Cat Missile Systems, 2 x 40mm guns, 6 Torpedo Tubes, 1 Lynx helicopter **Complement** 230.

**Notes**
The highly successful Leander Class are the last steam powered frigates in the Royal Navy, all later ships being propelled by gas turbines. Some vessels of this class are being refitted with the latest Towed Array sonar. Their armament has been reduced to 2 Sea Cat systems and the 40mm guns replaced by 20mm.

HMS Active

## AMAZON CLASS (Type 21)

| Ship | Pennant Number | Completion Date | Builder |
|---|---|---|---|
| AMAZON | F169 | 1974 | Vosper T. |
| ACTIVE | F171 | 1977 | Vosper T. |
| AMBUSCADE | F172 | 1975 | Yarrow |
| ARROW | F173 | 1976 | Yarrow |
| ALACRITY | F174 | 1977 | Yarrow |
| AVENGER | F185 | 1978 | Yarrow |

**Displacement** 3,250 tons **Dimensions** 117m x 13m x 6m **Speed** 30 knots **Armament** 1 x 4.5″ gun, 2 x 20mm guns, 4 Exocet Missiles, 1 Sea Cat Missile System, 1 Wasp/Lynx helicopter **Complement** 170.

**Notes**
Most of the class now have 6 torpedo tubes each. These General Purpose frigates were built to a commercial design by Vosper/Yarrow and subsequently sold to the Ministry of Defence. All of the class are being given extra hull strengthening (see photo).

HMS Yarmouth

## ROTHESAY CLASS (Type 12)

| Ship | Pennant Number | Completion Date | Builder |
|---|---|---|---|
| YARMOUTH | F101 | 1960 | J. Brown |
| LOWESTOFT | F103 | 1961 | Stephen |
| ROTHESAY | F107 | 1960 | Yarrow |
| FALMOUTH | F113 | 1961 | Swan Hunter |
| BERWICK | F115 | 1961 | Harland & Wolff |
| PLYMOUTH | F126 | 1961 | HM Dockyard Devonport |

**Displacement** 2,800 tons **Dimensions** 113m x 13m x 5m **Speed** 30 knots **Armament** 2 x 4.5″ guns, up to 4 x 20mm guns, 1 Sea Cat Missile System, 1 Mortar Mk10, 1 Wasp helicopter **Complement** 250.

**Notes**
All ships of this class were follow-on ships to the Whitby Class and then converted to carry a helicopter.
Plans to retire most of the class have been modified since the Falkland crisis. FALMOUTH will become a Harbour training ship in 1985. ROTHESAY is now expected to remain in the fleet until 1988.

HMS Torquay

## TYPE 12 (Trials Ships)

| Ship | Pennant Number | Completion Date | Builder |
|---|---|---|---|
| TORQUAY | F43 | 1956 | Harland & Wolff |

**Displacement** 2,800 tons **Dimensions** 112m x 12m x 5m **Speed** 29 knots **Armament** 2 x 4.5″ guns, 1 Mortar Mk10 **Complement** 250.

**Notes**
TORQUAY is a Navigational Training Ship but will be relieved by JUNO in mid 1985.

HMS Brecon

## MINE COUNTERMEASURES SHIPS (MCMV'S)
## BRECON CLASS

| Ship | Pennant Number | Builder |
|---|---|---|
| BRECON | M29 | Vosper T. |
| LEDBURY | M30 | Vosper T. |
| CATTISTOCK | M31 | Vosper T. |
| COTTESMORE | M32 | Yarrow |
| BROCKLESBY | M33 | Vosper T. |
| MIDDLETON | M34 | Yarrow |
| DULVERTON | M35 | Vosper T. |
| ATHERSTONE | M36 | Vosper T. |
| CHIDDINGFOLD | M37 | Vosper T. |
| BICESTER | M38 | Vosper T. |
| HURWORTH | M39 | Vosper T. |

**Displacement** 625 tonnes **Dimensions** 60m x 10m x 2.2m **Speed** 17 knots **Armament** 1 x 40mm gun **Complement** 45.

**Notes**
A new class of MCMV being built, albeit in small numbers, to replace the ageing Coniston Class over the next few years. The largest Warships ever to be built in Glass Reinforced Plastic. First nine in service—remainder building.

HMS Bickington

## CONISTON CLASS

| Ship | Penn. No. | Ship | Penn. No. |
|---|---|---|---|
| *ALFRISTON (S) | M1103 | *KEDLESTON (H) | M1153 |
| §BICKINGTON (S) | M1109 | *KELLINGTON (H) | M1154 |
| BILDESTON (H) | M1110 | KIRKLISTON (H) | M1157 |
| *BRERETON (H) | M1113 | MAXTON (H) | M1165 |
| BRINTON (H) | M1114 | NURTON (H) | M1166 |
| BRONINGTON (H) | M1115 | §POLLINGTON (S) | M1173 |
| WILTON (H) | M1116 | *SHAVINGTON (S) ● | M1180 |
| §CRICHTON (S) | M1124 | SHERATON (H) | M1181 |
| *CUXTON (S) | M1125 | §UPTON (S) ● | M1187 |
| BOSSINGTON (H) | M1133 | §WALKERTON (S) | M1188 |
| GAVINTON (H) | M1140 | *WOTTON (S) ● | M1195 |
| *HODGESTON (S) | M1146 | §SOBERTON (S) | M1200 |
| HUBBERSTON (H) | M1147 | §STUBBINGTON (S) | M1204 |
| IVESTON (H) | M1151 | | |

HMS Bronington

**CONISTON CLASS** (Cont.)

**Displacement** 425 tons **Dimensions** 46m x 9m x 3m **Speed** 15 knots **Armament** 1 x 40mm gun, 2 x 20mm guns (removed in some ships) **Complement** 29/38.

**Notes**

120 of this class were built in the early 50s but most have now been sold overseas or scrapped. They have fulfilled many roles over the years and have given excellent service. WILTON, built of glassfibre in 1973, was the world's first 'plastic' warship. Ships marked * are sea training tenders for the RNR. Ships marked § are employed on Coastal Fishery Protection duties. Ships marked (S) are Minesweepers — (H) Minehunters. GLASSERTON (M1141) in temporary use as a static RNR Training Ship on the Thames.

● Due to pay off 1985/6.

HMS Waveney

## FLEET MINESWEEPERS
## RIVER CLASS

| Ship | Pennant Number | Completion Date | Builder |
|---|---|---|---|
| WAVENEY | M2003 | 1984 | Richards |
| CARRON | M2004 | 1984 | Richards |
| DOVEY | M2005 | 1984 | Richards |
| HELFORD | M2006 | 1984 | Richards |
| HUMBER | M2007 | | Richards |
| BLACKWATER | M2008 | | Richards |
| ITCHEN | M2009 | | Richards |
| HELMSDALE | M2010 | | Richards |
| ORWELL | M2011 | | Richards |
| RIBBLE | M2012 | | Richards |
| SPEY | M2013 | | Richards |
| ARUN | M2014 | | Richards |

**Displacement** 850 tons **Dimensions** 47m x 10m x 3m **Speed** 14 knots **Armament** 2 x GPMG **Complement** 30.

**Notes**
All will replace Coastal Minesweepers in the RNR. Fitted for, but not with, 40mm gun.

HMS Abdiel

**MINELAYER**
**ABDIEL CLASS**

| Ship | Pennant Number | Completion Date | Builder |
|---|---|---|---|
| ABDIEL | N21 | 1967 | Thornycroft |

**Displacement** 1,500 tons **Dimensions** 80m x 13m x 4m **Speed** 16 knots **Armament** 44 mines. 1 x 40mm gun**Complement** 77.

**Notes**
Designed as a Headquarters and Support Ship for minecounter-measure forces and exercise minelayer. Workshops & spares embarked enable minecountermeasures ships to operate well away from home bases.
ABDIEL is the only operational minelayer in the Royal Navy but plans exist to use merchant ships to lay mines if required.

**HMS Leeds Castle**

## CASTLE CLASS

| Ship | Pennant Number | Completion Date | Builder |
|---|---|---|---|
| LEEDS CASTLE | P258 | 1981 | Hall Russell |
| DUMBARTON CASTLE | P265 | 1982 | Hall Russell |

**Displacement** 1,450 tons **Dimensions** 81m x 11m x 3m **Speed** 20 knots **Armament** 1 x 40mm gun. **Complement** 40.

**Notes**
These ships have a dual role—that of fishery protection and off-shore patrols within the limits of UK territorial waters—no less than 270,000 sq miles! Unlike the Island Class these ships are able to operate helicopters—including Sea King aircraft. Trials have been conducted to assess the suitability of these ships as Minelayers. The 40mm gun could be replaced by the Oto Melara 76mm if required.

HMS Guernsey

## ISLAND CLASS

| Ship | Pennant Number | Completion Date | Builder |
|---|---|---|---|
| ANGLESEY | P277 | 1979 | Hall Russell |
| ALDERNEY | P278 | 1979 | Hall Russell |
| JERSEY | P295 | 1976 | Hall Russell |
| GUERNSEY | P297 | 1977 | Hall Russell |
| SHETLAND | P298 | 1977 | Hall Russell |
| ORKNEY | P299 | 1977 | Hall Russell |
| LINDISFARNE | P300 | 1978 | Hall Russell |

**Displacement** 1,250 tons **Dimensions** 60m x 11m x 4m **Speed** 17 knots **Armament** 1 x 40mm gun **Complement** 39.

**Notes**
Built on trawler lines these ships were introduced to protect the extensive British interests in North Sea oil installations and to patrol the 200 mile fishery limit.

The Hong Kong Squadron

## PATROL BOATS

| Ship | Pennant Number | Completion Date | Builder |
|---|---|---|---|
| BEACHAMPTON | P1007 | 1953 | Goole SB |
| MONKTON | P1055 | 1956 | Herd Mackenzie |
| WASPERTON | P1089 | 1956 | J.S. White |
| WOLVERTON | P1093 | 1957 | Montrose SYCo. |
| YARNTON | P1096 | 1956 | Pickersgill |

**Displacement** 425 tons **Dimensions** 46m x 9m x 3m **Speed** 15 knots **Armament** 2 x 40mm guns **Complement** 32.

**Notes**
Former Coastal Minesweepers converted to Patrol Boats in 1971 for service in Hong Kong. Conversion involved removal of most minesweeping equipment and fitting extra 40mm gun aft of the funnel. All will gradually be retired as Peacock Class enter service in Hong Kong during 1985.

HMS Peacock

## PEACOCK CLASS

| Ship | Pennant Number | Completion Date | Builder |
|---|---|---|---|
| PEACOCK | P239 | 1983 | Hall Russell |
| PLOVER | P240 | 1983 | Hall Russell |
| STARLING | P241 | 1984 | Hall Russell |
| SWALLOW | P242 | 1984 | Hall Russell |
| SWIFT | P243 | 1984 | Hall Russell |

**Displacement** 700 tons **Dimensions** 60m x 10m x 5m **Speed** 28 knots **Armament** 1 x 76mm gun **Complement** 31.

**Notes**
The first two ships have arrived in Hong Kong to replace two of the ageing Ton class Patrol Vessels. They are the first RN warships to carry the 76mm Oto Melara gun. Considerably faster vessels than those they are to replace, they will be used to provide an ocean going back-up to the Marine Department of the Hong Kong Police. The Government of Hong Kong has paid 75% of the building and maintenance costs of these vessels.

**HMS Guardian**

| Ship | Pennant Number | Completion Date | Builder |
|---|---|---|---|
| PROTECTOR | P244 | 1975 | Drypool Selby |
| GUARDIAN | P245 | 1975 | Beverley |
| SENTINEL | P246 | 1975 | Husumwerft |

**Displacement** 802 tons **Speed** 14 knots **Armament** 2 x 40mm **Complement** 24/6.

**Notes**
Formerly Oil Rig support vessels Seaforth Saga, Seaforth Champion and Seaforth Warrior (respectively) purchased from Seaforth Maritime Ltd. They are permanent Falkland Island Patrol Vessels.
GUARDIAN varies slightly from the other two vessels.

Artist's impression

**Coastal Training Craft**

A contract for fourteen 20 metre Coastal Training craft was awarded to Watercraft Ltd in June 1984. The craft will replace existing vessels at present operated by the Royal Naval Reserve, RN University Units & the RNXS. They will be powered by two 650shp diesel engines — providing a speed in excess of 20 knots.

The first of the class will be delivered in April/May 1985.

## TRAINING SHIPS

| Ship | Pennant Number | Completion Date | Builder |
|---|---|---|---|
| WATERWITCH | M2720 | 1960 | J.S. White |
| WOODLARK | M2780 | 1959 | J.S. White |

**Displacement** 160 tons **Dimensions** 32m x 7m x 2m **Speed** 12 knots **Complement** 19.

**Notes**

Former Inshore Survey Craft now used as training ships for RN University units (WATERWITCH at Liverpool & WOODLARK at Southampton). Expected to be paid off by Spring 1985.

HMS Sandpiper

## BIRD CLASS

| Ship | Pennant Number | Completion Date | Builder |
|---|---|---|---|
| KINGFISHER | P260 | 1975 | R. Dunston |
| CYGNET | P261 | 1976 | R. Dunston |
| PETEREL | P262 | 1976 | R. Dunston |
| SANDPIPER | P263 | 1977 | R. Dunston |

**Displacement** 190 tons **Dimensions** 37m x 7m x 2m **Speed** 21 knots **Armament** 1 x 40mm gun **Complement** 24.

### Notes
Based on the RAF long range recovery vessels, these craft were built for fishery protection duties. They have not been very successful as they have proved to be bad seaboats. PETEREL and SANDPIPER are now used by Britannia Royal Naval College, Dartmouth, as training ships. The other two ships are employed on coastal patrol duties.

HMS Attacker

## ATTACKER CLASS

| Ship | Pennant Number | Completion Date | Builder |
|---|---|---|---|
| ATTACKER | P281 | 1983 | Allday |
| CHASER | P282 | 1984 | Allday |
| FENCER | P283 | 1983 | Allday |
| HUNTER | P284 | 1983 | Allday |
| STRIKER | P285 | 1984 | Allday |

**Displacement** 34 tons **Dimensions** 20m x 5m x 1m **Speed** 24 knots **Complement** 11.

**Notes**
New Seamanship & Navigational training vessels for the Royal Naval Reserve & University RN Units. Based on a successful design used by HM Customs.

**HMS Manly**

| Ship | Pennant Number | Completion Date | Builder |
|---|---|---|---|
| MANLY | A92 | 1982 | R. Dunston |
| MENTOR | A94 | 1982 | R. Dunston |
| MILBROOK | A97 | 1982 | R. Dunston |
| MESSINA | A107 | 1982 | R. Dunston |

**Displacement** 127 tons **Dimensions** 25m x 6m x 2m **Speed** 10 knots **Complement** 13.

**Notes**
Very similar to the RMAS/RNXS tenders. These four craft are all employed on training duties (first three named attached to HMS RALEIGH for new entry training). IXWORTH (A318), ETTRICK (A274), ELSING (A277), IRONBRIDGE (A311) & DATCHET (A357) are all former RMAS tenders now flying the White Ensign.

HMS Herald

## HECLA CLASS

| Ship | Pennant Number | Completion Date | Builder |
|---|---|---|---|
| HECLA | A133 | 1965 | Yarrow |
| HECATE | A137 | 1965 | Yarrow |
| HERALD | A138 | 1974 | Robb Caledon |
| HYDRA | A144 | 1966 | Yarrow |

**Displacement** 2,733 tons **Dimensions** 79m x 15m x 5m **Speed** 14 knots **Complement** 115.

**Notes**
Able to operate for long periods away from shore support, these ships and the smaller ships of the Hydrographic Fleet collect the data that is required to produce the Admiralty Charts and publications which are sold to mariners worldwide. Each ship usually carries a Wasp helicopter. HERALD is an improved version of the earlier ships and now operates in the South Atlantic when HMS ENDURANCE is not on station. In this role she is armed (2 x 20mm) and painted grey.

HMS Beagle

## BULLDOG CLASS

| Ship | Pennant Number | Completion Date | Builder |
|---|---|---|---|
| BULLDOG | A317 | 1968 | Brooke Marine |
| BEAGLE | A319 | 1968 | Brooke Marine |
| FOX | A320 | 1968 | Brooke Marine |
| FAWN | A335 | 1968 | Brooke Marine |

**Displacement** 1,088 tons **Dimensions** 60m x 11m x 4m **Speed** 15 knots **Complement** 39.

**Notes**
Designed to operate in coastal waters. An enlarged coastal survey vessel, to be named HMS ROEBUCK, has been ordered. It will cost £8 million and delivery is expected in early 1986.

HMS Enterprise

## INSHORE SURVEY CRAFT

| Ship | Pennant Number | Completion Date | Builder |
|---|---|---|---|
| ECHO | A70 | 1958 | J.S. White |
| ENTERPRISE | A71 | 1959 | M.W. Blackmore |
| EGERIA | A72 | 1959 | Wm Weatherhead |

**Displacement** 160 tons **Dimensions** 32m x 7m x 2m **Speed** 14 knots **Complement** 19.

**Notes**
Built for survey work in harbours and river estuaries. These craft are due to be paid off in 1985 but plans to replace them with a sidewall hovercraft have been abandoned. The 15 metre launch, HMS GLEANER (A86) was accepted into service in late 1983.

**HMS Challenger**

## SEABED OPERATIONS VESSEL

| Ship | Pennant Number | Completion Date | Builder |
|---|---|---|---|
| CHALLENGER | K07 | 1984 | Scott Lithgow |

**Displacement** 6,400 tons **Dimensions** 134m x 18m x 5m **Speed** 15 knots **Complement** 185.

**Notes**
CHALLENGER is equipped to find, inspect and, where appropriate, recover objects from the seabed at greater depths than is currently possible. She is designed with a saturation diving system enabling up to 12 men to live in comfort for long periods in a decompression chamber amidships, taking their turns to be lowered in a diving bell to work on the seabed. Also fitted to carry out salvage work. Until CHALLENGER has completed lengthy trials, the MV SEAFORTH CLANSMAN (3,300 tons) will remain on charter to the MoD for another 18 months - 2 years.

RFA Reliant

HMS Manchester

HMS Brocklesby

HMS Pollington

HMS Peacock

HMS Charybdis

RFA Black Rover (& HM Ships Bildeston & Cattistock)

RMAS Rollicker

HMY Britannia

## ROYAL YACHT

| Ship | Pennant Number | Completion Date | Builder |
|---|---|---|---|
| BRITANNIA | A00 | 1954 | J. Brown |

**Displacement** 4,961 tons **Dimensions** 126m x 17m x 5m **Speed** 21 knots **Complement** 270..

**Notes**
Probably the best known ship in the Royal Navy, BRITANNIA was designed to be converted to a hospital ship in time of war but this conversion was not made during the Falklands crisis. Is used for NATO exercises when not on 'Royal' business. Dark blue hull and buff funnel. Normally to be seen in Portsmouth Harbour when not away on official duties.

HMS Endurance

## ICE PATROL SHIP

| Ship | Pennant Number | Completion Date | Builder |
|---|---|---|---|
| ENDURANCE (ex MV Anita Dan) | A171 | 1956 | Krogerwerft Rendsburg |

**Displacement** 3,600 tons **Dimensions** 93m x 14m x 5m **Speed** 14 knots **Armament** 2 x 20mm guns **Complement** 124.

**Notes**
Purchased from Denmark in 1967 ENDURANCE is painted brilliant red for easy identification in the ice of Antarctica where she spends 6 months of the year. Her role is to undertake oceanographic and hydrographic surveys in the area and support scientists working ashore. A small Royal Marine detachment is embarked. Was to have been "retired early" after her 1982 season in Antarctica, but reprieved as a result of the Falklands crisis. To undergo major refit in 1985/6.

HMS Wakeful

## TUG/SUBMARINE TENDER

| Ship | Pennant Number | Builder |
| --- | --- | --- |
| WAKEFUL (Ex Dan) | A236 | Cochranes |

**Displacement** 900 tons **Dimensions** 44m x 11m x 5m **Speed** 14 knots **Complement** 25.

**Notes**
Purchased from Swedish owners in 1974 for duties in the Clyde area as Submarine Target Ship and at the Clyde Submarine Base —HMS NEPTUNE. Has been used for Fishery Protection work and the shadowing of Soviet warships in British waters. The trawler NORTHELLA—converted for service as a Minesweeper during the Falklands conflict has been chartered for service in the Clyde area for submarine escort duties.

# THE ROYAL FLEET AUXILIARY

The Royal Fleet Auxiliary Service is operated by the Director of Supplies & Transport (Ships and Fuel) whose directorate forms part of the Royal Navy Supply and Transport Service (RNSTS) within the Ministry of Defence. The RNSTS provides the total logistic support of the Royal Navy and is civilian manned throughout under the management of the Director General of Supplies & Transport (Navy).

All Royal Fleet Auxiliaries are manned by merchant navy personnel and operate under their own distinctive flag—a blue ensign with a verticle anchor in gold on the fly, which distinguishes them from other non-commissioned ships and craft engaged in the naval service. All officers, and a growing proportion of ratings, serve under contract to the Royal Fleet Auxiliary Service.

The ships, all painted grey and looking in every respect "warlike", are shortly to become armed—all the larger RFAs have carried guns either mounted on deck—or crated in the holds—in recent years. Largely as a result of the Falklands conflict, all RFAs will be fitted with "self defence" anti-aircraft armament during the next 12 months.

For years Royal Fleet Auxiliaries have been able to enter foreign ports using their merchant ship status, without giving the authorities advance notice—a privilege not afforded to any warship—of any nation. This facility has frequently been useful to a naval task force commander who, needing stores or mail collected or urgent medical and welfare cases landed, has been able to despatch an RFA to the nearest port at no notice. With more and more RFAs carrying helicopters and now appearing with light armament too, it has become beyond the limit of credibility to say these ships are "simple merchantmen".

For a number of years overseas governments have been advised of the arrival of an RFA in local waters and an announcement is expected shortly to change the whole status of the service. It is expected that the whole Fleet will be "deregistered" and, instead of sailing as merchantmen, sail as government vessels. Outwardly not a lot will change—ports of registry will disappear from the sterns of ships of the Fleet and before any RFA visits a foreign port, full diplomatic clearance will have to be obtained. One advantage will be that it will be easier for RFAs to embark service personnel as passengers. In the past, to do so has generated a pile of paperwork as officially these vessels have only been certified to carry a small number of passengers—in a similar fashion to a coastal merchantman, a situation far from satisfactory for the Navy, RFA & merchant authorities. The change of status of these ships will mean they loose the right to simply arrive without notice in foreign ports. It will be interesting to see what effect, if any, this has on the Fleet's ability to operate away from United Kingdom waters.

As has widely been reported, the Ministry has asked a number of defence contractors to design the "one stop" RFA of the 1990s. This ship would carry the full range of stores required by the Fleet—fuel, oil, ammunition & a wide range of air, naval and victualling items. The concept has long been discussed—it has obvious advantages in saving manpower in the Fleet—but cries of putting all one's eggs in one (very explosive) basket are also frequently heard. The ability of one ship to only be in one place at one time are obvious—the lack of flexibility with the RFA Fleet will be a penalty that will have to be paid if the "big is beautiful" policy is to be adopted for the future Fleet. Time will tell if such a ship will ever be built. It is interesting to note that no mention has been made regarding which service will man these proposed vessels—it could well be visualised that they fly the white ensign and be what they are in all respect but name—warships.

After the "diversion" to Beirut, RFA Reliant is now in South Atlantic waters and it will be interesting to see how she performs in the role for which she was purchased. The concept was to convert a merchant ship, in a matter of days, into a mini aircraft "carrier" to be sailed, or even towed, to an operating area. There is a major difference in a converted merchant ship being able to carry, as opposed to operate, aircraft and the "Reliant experiment" where she has been used to operate aircraft—in open sea conditions—has not been good. Her light hull has made her lively in relatively calm weather and her construction has meant aircraft on deck have been drenched by salt water spray on many occasions.

A highly active deck and salt water corrosion are not condusive to good helicopter operations! If she remains close inshore around the Falklands, she could be a most useful asset in the area—if she is given a "deep sea" role it could be a very different story.

The other merchant ship to appear in RFA colours in the recent past—RFA Diligence—seems to be a "good buy". Her ability to act as a depot and repair ship in the Falklands seems to be working well. Operating ships, which are being worked hard, so far from home, demands a lot of back up services—those provided by Diligence are vital to keep the Falklands force fighting fit.

While the Ol & Tide Class tankers keep the Falkland Task Group supplied with fuel and stores, the Leaf Class tankers are deployed with the RN ships in the Indian Ocean and Gulf Patrol.

Whichever flag they fly or how the paperwork is run—matters not. The ships and men of the Royal Fleet Auxiliary perform an Increasingly important role in the Navy's worldwide operating capability—a task more vital now than it has ever been.

## SHIPS OF THE ROYAL FLEET AUXILIARY
### Pennant Numbers

| Ship | Penn. No. | Ship | Penn. No. |
|---|---|---|---|
| TIDESPRING | A75 | GOLD ROVER | A271 |
| PEARLEAF | A77 | BLACK ROVER | A273 |
| PLUMLEAF | A78 | FORT GRANGE | A385 |
| APPLELEAF | A79 | FORT AUSTIN | A386 |
| BRAMBLELEAF | A81 | RESOURCE | A480 |
| BAYLEAF | A109 | REGENT | A486 |
| ORANGELEAF | A110 | ENGADINE | K08 |
| OLWEN | A122 | SIR BEDIVERE | L3004 |
| OLNA | A123 | SIR GERAINT | L3027 |
| OLMEDA | A124 | SIR LANCELOT | L3029 |
| RELIANT | A131 | SIR PERCIVALE | L3036 |
| DILIGENCE | A132 | SIR TRISTRAM | L3505 |
| GREEN ROVER | A268 | SIR CARADOC | L3522 |
| GREY ROVER | A269 | SIR LAMORAK | L3532 |
| BLUE ROVER | A270 | | |

**RFA Reliant**

| Ship | Pennant Number | Completion Date | Builder |
|---|---|---|---|
| RELIANT | A131 | 1977 | Gdansk Poland |

**Displacement** 27,867 tons **Dimensions** 204m x 31m x 9m **Speed** 21 knots **Armament** 4 x 20mm + 5 Sea King Helicopters **Complement** 61 (RFA) + 150 (RN).

**Notes**
The former merchant ship M/V Astronomer, taken up from trade during the Falklands War—refitted during 1983 with the US Arapaho system. She now provides additional helicopter operating capability and stores support in South Atlantic waters.

RFA Olwen

## 'OL' CLASS

| Ship | Pennant Number | Completion Date | Builder |
|---|---|---|---|
| OLWEN | A122 | 1965 | Hawthorn Leslie |
| OLNA | A123 | 1966 | Hawthorn Leslie |
| OLMEDA | A124 | 1965 | Swan Hunter |

**Displacement** 36,000 tons **Dimensions** 197m x 26m x 10m **Speed** 19 knots **Complement** 94.

**Notes**
These ships can carry up to 3 Wessex helicopters. Dry stores can be carried—and transferred at sea—as well as a wide range of fuel, aviation spirit and lubricants.

RFA Tidespring

## TIDE CLASS

| Ship | Pennant Number | Completion Date | Builder |
|---|---|---|---|
| TIDESPRING | A75 | 1963 | Hawthorn Leslie |

**Displacement** 27,400 tons **Dimensions** 177m x 22m x 10m **Speed** 18 knots **Complement** 110.

**Notes**
Built to fuel warships at sea in any part of the world including strengthening for ice operations. A hangar and flight deck provides space for three Wessex helicopters if required. Was due to be "retired early" during 1982/3. But reprieved for Falklands crisis. TIDEPOOL sold to Chile 1982.

RFA Black Rover

## ROVER CLASS

| Ship | Pennant Number | Completion Date | Builder |
|---|---|---|---|
| GREEN ROVER | A268 | 1969 | Swan Hunter |
| GREY ROVER | A269 | 1970 | Swan Hunter |
| BLUE ROVER | A270 | 1970 | Swan Hunter |
| GOLD ROVER | A271 | 1974 | Swan Hunter |
| BLACK ROVER | A273 | 1974 | Swan Hunter |

**Displacement** 11,522 tons **Dimensions** 141m x 19m x 7m **Speed** 18 knots **Complement** 50.

**Notes**
Small Fleet Tankers designed to supply HM ships with fresh water, dry cargo and refrigerated provisions as well as a range of fuel and lubricants.

RFA Bayleaf

## LEAF CLASS (New)

| Ship | Pennant Number | Completion Date | Builder |
|---|---|---|---|
| APPLELEAF | A79 | 1980 | Cammell Laird |
| BRAMBLELEAF | A81 | 1980 | Cammell Laird |
| BAYLEAF | A109 | 1982 | Cammell Laird |
| ORANGELEAF | A110 | 1982 | Cammell Laird |

**Displacement** 37,747 tons **Dimensions** 170m x 26m x 12m **Speed** 14.5 knots **Complement** 60.

**Notes**
APPLELEAF and BRAMBLELEAF are ex Merchant Vessels (Hudson Deep and Hudson Cavalier) taken over by the Ministry when part completed. BAYLEAF is a sister ship owned by Lombard North Central Ltd and on charter to MoD. ORANGE-LEAF is the former M/V BALDER LONDON.

RFA Pearleaf

## LEAF CLASS (Old)

| Ship | Pennant Number | Completion Date | Builder |
|---|---|---|---|
| PEARLEAF | A77 | 1960 | Blythwood |
| PLUMLEAF | A78 | 1960 | Blyth D.D. |

**Displacement** Both about 25,000 tons **Dimensions** 170m x 22m x 7m **Speed** 15 knots **Complement** 55.

**Notes**
These 2 different ships are on long term charter to the Ministry of Defence from their civilian owners and are employed on freighting duties between oil terminals, but have limited replenished facilities to fuel HM ships at sea. Both due to have been deleted from RFA Fleet but reprieved by Falklands crisis. Both expected to be retired during 1985/6.

RFA Fort Grange

## FORT CLASS

| Ship | Pennant Number | Completion Date | Builder |
|---|---|---|---|
| FORT GRANGE | A385 | 1978 | Scott Lithgow |
| FORT AUSTIN | A386 | 1979 | Scott Lithgow |

**Displacement** 17,000 tons **Dimensions** 183m x 24m x 9m **Speed** 20 knots **Complement** 133.

**Notes**
Full hangar and maintenance facilities are provided and up to four Sea King helicopters can be carried for both the transfer of stores and anti-submarine protection of a group of ships. Both are armed when in the South Atlantic. 2 x 20mm guns are mounted on the Scot platforms.

RFA Regent

## REGENT CLASS

| Ship | Pennant Number | Completion Date | Builder |
|---|---|---|---|
| RESOURCE | A480 | 1967 | Scotts |
| REGENT | A486 | 1967 | Harland & Wolff |

**Displacement** 22,890 **Dimensions** 195m x 24m x 8m **Speed** 21 knots **Complement** 123.

**Notes**
The only RFA ships with an RN helicopter permanently embarked for supplying ships with a full range of the Naval Armament stores and ammunition carried aboard. A limited range of Naval Stores and food is also carried.

RFA Sir Bedivere

## LANDING SHIPS
## SIR LANCELOT CLASS

| Ship | Pennant Number | Completion Date | Builder |
|---|---|---|---|
| SIR BEDIVERE | L3004 | 1967 | Hawthorn |
| SIR GERAINT | L3027 | 1967 | Stephen |
| SIR LANCELOT | L3029 | 1964 | Fairfield |
| SIR PERCIVALE | L3036 | 1968 | Hawthorn |

**Displacement** 5,550 tons **Dimensions** 126m x 18m x 4m **Speed** 17 knots **Armament** Can be fitted with 2 x 40mm guns in emergency **Complement** 69.

**Notes**
Manned by the RFA but tasked by the Army, these ships are used for heavy transport of stores—embarked by bow and stern doors—and beach assault landings. Can operate helicopters from tank deck if required. SIR TRISTRAM is being rebuilt (with additional 29ft section) after Falklands War damage. A replacement for SIR GALAHAD has been ordered.

**RFA Sir Lamorak**

| Ship | Pennant Number | Completion Date | Builder |
|---|---|---|---|
| SIR CARADOC | L3522 | 1973 | Trosvik Verksted |
| SIR LAMORAK | L3532 | 1972 | Ankerlokken Verft |

**Displacement** 3,350 tons (Lamorak 2,566) **Dimensions** 124m (Lamorak 108m) x 16 (Lamorak 20m) **Speed** 14 knots (17 knots Lamorak) **Complement** 24.

**Notes**
Sir Caradoc is ex Grey Master and Sir Lamorak is ex Lakespan Ontario. Both are on charter from their civilian owners as "stop gap" replacements for Sir Tristram and Sir Galahad. Sir Lamorak is likely to be returned to her own civilian owners in 1985.

Found to be unsuitable for operations in the South Atlantic and now employed on the Marchwood/Antwerp freight run for MoD (Army).

RFA Diligence

| Ship | Pennant Number | Completion Date | Builder |
|---|---|---|---|
| DILIGENCE | A132 | 1981 | Oresundsvarvet |

**Displacement** 5,814 tons **Dimensions** 120m x 12m **Speed** 15 knots **Complement** RFA 40. RN Personnel — approx 100.

**Notes**
Formerly the M/V Stena Inspector purchased (£25m) for service in the South Atlantic. Accommodation is provided for up to 100 men from a Fleet Maintenance Unit to be embarked. Her deep diving complex has been removed & workshops added.

**RFA Engadine**

| Ship | Pennant Number | Completion Date | Builder |
|---|---|---|---|
| ENGADINE | K08 | 1967 | Robb |

**Displacement** 9,000 tons **Dimensions** 129m x 17m x 7m **Speed** 16 knots **Complement** 73 (+ RN group).

**Notes**
Specially built for RFA service (but with embarked RN personnel) to provide training ship for helicopter crews operating in deep waters well away from coasts. Can operate up to 6 helicopters and often embarks pilotless target aircraft for exercises. Hangar for them above main hangar. A merchant vessel (M/V Contender Bezant) is being rebuilt at Belfast as an eventual replacement for this ship in 1986/7.

# ROYAL MARITIME AUXILIARY SERVICE

The Royal Maritime Auxiliary Service Fleet is comprised of 530 hulls, of which 330 are self propelled, including small harbour launches, the remainder being dumb craft such as lighters etc. It is administered by the Director of Marine Services (Naval) to whom the Captains of the Ports and Resident Naval Officers at the various Naval Bases are mainly responsible for the provision of Marine Services to the Royal Navy. The RMAS also provides many types of craft for the numerous and diverse requirements of other Ministry of Defence departments.

Ships of the RMAS, which can be seen at work in all the Naval Bases throughout the United Kingdom and at Gibraltar, are easily identified by their black hulls, buff coloured superstructure and funnels, and by the RMAS flag, which is a blue ensign defaced in the fly by a yellow anchor over two wavy lines. Pennant numbers are painted only on those vessels that are normally employed outside harbour limits.

The largest section of the fleet is employed on harbour duties, the types of vessels involved being Harbour tugs, Fleet Tenders, Tank Cleaning Lighters, Harbour Launches, Naval Armament Vessels and dumb lighters for carrying ammunition, general stores, fuel, water and victuals to the Royal Navy, NATO Navies and Royal Fleet Auxiliary ships when they are in port or at anchor. In keeping with the Director of Marine Services policy of multi-role vessels, many of the larger units of the fleet have been modified to back up the harbour fleet when required.

A smaller section of the fleet is, however, engaged in a purely sea-going capacity. Ocean Tugs, Torpedo Recovery Vessels and Mooring and Salvage Vessels are designed and equipped for world wide towing and complex Marine Salvage operations. Experimental Trials Vessels, fitted with some of the most sophisticated modern equipment, are deployed on a wide range of duties in the fast growing area of advanced experimental technology necessary for the design of new warships, weapons systems and machinery.

Oil pollution has become more prevalent, and to deal with emergencies in Dockyard Ports or to assist the Department of Transport with those that may arise around the coastline of the United Kingdom, the RMAS has adapted many of its vessels to carry dispersant chemicals and the necessary spraying equipment. This task will become more important as stricter International Laws come into force governing the prevention of pollution of coastal waters by all ships.

1983 saw a cutback in the RMAS Fleet, brought about, in the main, by the closure of the Naval Base at Chatham and the change in the roles of certain of the remaining Naval Bases. Older units of the Fleet have been disposed of without replacement and the introduction of new "multi-role" vessels will continue to provide a saving in the number of ships required in the Fleet.

Changes in the size and shape of the RMAS Fleet will continue in the future and will be compatible with the changing needs of the Royal Navy which it exists to serve.

Throughout 1984 studies have been undertaken on the future role of the RMAS. With the decision already made, by the Government, to disband the marine branch of the Royal Air Force, attention turned to the future role and requirement for the RMAS as it is currently known.

Much speculation—informed and otherwise—has been seen on how the service will look in the future—and a decision is expected in the very near future. The words of cuts, contractors, privatisation and redundancies have been banded about frequently. No doubt there is a future for all these—but one hopes all the implications of cutting and commercialising the service have been investigated in depth. MoD contracts for small ship support will attract many hopeful bidders and the savings they could bring to the MoD could be considerable—there are still branches of the RMAS tree that can be pruned without major effect on the Fleet. However, contrators may not be the answer for a military support service when, in some areas, an instant response (not exactly defined by contract) is required. There is undoubted loyalty within the RMAS and the service given is good—albeit expensive. Being a civil service organisation the Fleet sails on its paperwork—all of which is expensive in both time, money and manpower.

With labour intensive ships such as the St Margarets paying off —without replacement—jobs are being cut. Already chartered merchant ships of trawler size—and very small crews—are appearing to carry out tasks previously undertaken by RMAS ships. Undoubtedly this is being seen as the writing on the wall. For security reasons alone, the ships engaged on trials and research must continue under full government control. No doubt the harbour tug, fuel, water and "barge business" will be an attractive proposition to be placed with a commercial contractor, whilst those in the service expect the deep sea tugs to either suffer a similar "fate"—or return to their original operators—the RFA. The fate of the Admiralty pilots—who also command the large tugs—is also very much in the melting pot.

1984 has been a year of uncertainty throughout the RMAS—the sooner a decision can be made on its future the better. Rumour is rife, which is neither good for the service or the customer . . . the Royal Navy Fleet which it is designed to serve.

During 1984 the following deletions from the RMAS Fleet were made:

AIREDALE—to commercial service at Gibraltar
ADVICE—For disposal
ST MARGARETS—For disposal Dec '84.
LAYMOOR—For disposal Nov '84.

## SHIPS OF THE ROYAL MARITIME AUXILIARY SERVICE — PENNANT NUMBERS

| Ship | Penn. No. | Ship | Penn. No. |
|---|---|---|---|
| MELTON | A83 | ACCORD | A90 |
| MENAI | A84 | MILFORD | A91 |
| MEON | A87 | TYPHOON | A95 |
| AGILE | A88 | BEAULIEU | A99 |

| Ship | Penn. No. | Ship | Penn. No. |
|---|---|---|---|
| BEDDGELERT | A100 | MARY | A175 |
| BEMBRIDGE | A101 | EDITH | A177 |
| BIBURY | A103 | HUSKY | A178 |
| BLAKENEY | A104 | MASTIFF | A180 |
| BRODICK | A105 | IRENE | A181 |
| ALSATIAN | A106 | SALUKI | A182 |
| FELICITY | A112 | ISABEL | A183 |
| MAGNET | A114 | POINTER | A188 |
| LODESTONE | A115 | SETTER | A189 |
| CAIRN | A126 | JOAN | A190 |
| TORRENT | A127 | JOYCE | A193 |
| TORRID | A128 | GWENDOLINE | A196 |
| DALMATIAN | A129 | SEALYHAM | A197 |
| TORNADO | A140 | HELEN | A198 |
| TORCH | A141 | MYRTLE | A199 |
| TORMENTOR | A142 | SPANIEL | A201 |
| TOREADOR | A143 | NANCY | A202 |
| DAISY | A145 | NORAH | A205 |
| WATERMAN | A146 | LLANDOVERY | A207 |
| FRANCES | A147 | LAMLASH | A208 |
| FIONA | A148 | CHARLOTTE | A210 |
| FLORENCE | A149 | LECHLADE | A211 |
| GENEVIEVE | A150 | ENDEAVOUR | A213 |
| GEORGINA | A152 | BEE | A216 |
| DEERHOUND | A155 | CHRISTINE | A217 |
| DAPHNE | A156 | CLARE | A218 |
| LOYAL HELPER | A157 | LOYAL MODERATOR | A220 |
| SUPPORTER | A158 | FORCEFUL | A221 |
| LOYAL WATCHER | A159 | NIMBLE | A222 |
| LOYAL VOLUNTEER | A160 | POWERFUL | A223 |
| LOYAL MEDIATOR | A161 | ADEPT | A224 |
| ELKHOUND | A162 | BUSTLER | A225 |
| GOOSANDER | A164 | CAPABLE | A226 |
| POCHARD | A165 | CAREFUL | A227 |
| KATHLEEN | A166 | FAITHFUL | A228 |
| LABRADOR | A168 | CRICKET | A229 |
| KITTY | A170 | COCKCHAFER | A230 |
| LESLEY | A172 | DEXTEROUS | A231 |
| DOROTHY | A173 | KINGARTH | A232 |
| LILAH | A174 | | |

| Ship | Penn. No. | Ship | Penn. No. |
|---|---|---|---|
| GNAT | A239 | KINLOSS | A482 |
| SHEEPDOG | A250 | CROMARTY | A488 |
| DORIS | A252 | DORNOCH | A490 |
| LADYBIRD | A253 | ROLLICKER | A502 |
| CICALA | A263 | UPLIFTER | A507 |
| SCARAB | A272 | HEADCORN | A1766 |
| KINBRACE | A281 | HEVER | A1767 |
| AURICULA | A285 | HARLECH | A1768 |
| CONFIDENT | A290 | HAMBLEDON | A1769 |
| ILCHESTER | A308 | LOYAL CHANCELLOR | A1770 |
| INSTOW | A309 | LOYAL PROCTOR | A1771 |
| FOXHOUND | A326 | HOLMWOOD | A1772 |
| BASSET | A327 | HORNING | A1773 |
| COLLIE | A328 | SHIPHAM | M2726 |
| CORGI | A330 | PORTISHAM | M2781 |
| FOTHERBY | A341 | SANDRINGHAM | M2791 |
| FELSTEAD | A348 | MANDARIN | P192 |
| CARTMEL | A350 | PINTAIL | P193 |
| CAWSAND | A351 | GARGANEY | P194 |
| ELKSTONE | A353 | GOLDENEYE | P195 |
| FROXFIELD | A354 | ABERDOVEY | Y10 |
| EPWORTH | A355 | ABINGER | Y11 |
| DATCHET | A357 | ALNESS | Y12 |
| ROYSTERER | A361 | ALNMOUTH | Y13 |
| DOLWEN | A362 | ASHCOTT | Y16 |
| DENMEAD | A363 | WATERFALL | Y17 |
| WHITEHEAD | A364 | WATERSHED | Y18 |
| FULBECK | A365 | WATERSPOUT | Y19 |
| ROBUST | A366 | WATERSIDE | Y20 |
| NEWTON | A367 | OILPRESS | Y21 |
| KINTERBURY | A378 | OILSTONE | Y22 |
| THROSK | A379 | OILWELL | Y23 |
| CRICKLADE | A381 | OILFIELD | Y24 |
| APPLEBY | A383 | OILBIRD | Y25 |
| CLOVELLY | A389 | OILMAN | Y26 |
| CRICCIETH | A391 | WATERCOURSE | Y30 |
| GLENCOE | A392 | WATERFOWL | Y31 |
| DUNSTER | A393 | | |
| FINTRY | A394 | | |
| GRASMERE | A402 | | |

RMAS Robust

## ROYSTERER CLASS

| Ship | Pennant Number | Completion Date | Builder |
|---|---|---|---|
| ROYSTERER | A361 | 1972 | C.D. Holmes |
| ROBUST | A366 | 1974 | C.D. Holmes |
| ROLLICKER | A502 | 1973 | C.D. Holmes |

**G.R.T.** 1,036 tons **Dimensions** 54m x 12m x 6m **Speed** 15 knots **Complement** 28.

**Notes**
Built for salvage and long range towage, but are also used for harbour duties.

RMAS Typhoon

## TYPHOON CLASS

| Ship | Pennant Number | Completion Date | Bullder |
|---|---|---|---|
| TYPHOON | A95 | 1960 | Henry Robb |

**G.R.T.** 1,034 tons **Dimensions** 60m x 12m x 4m **Speed** 17 knots **Complement** 27.

**Notes**
Long range towage and salvage tug. Now based at Greenock.

RMAS Accord

## CONFIANCE CLASS

| Ship | Pennant Number | Completion Date | Builder |
|---|---|---|---|
| AGILE | A88 | 1959 | Goole SB Co. |
| ACCORD | A90 | 1958 | A & J Inglis |
| CONFIDENT | A290 | 1956 | A & J Inglis |

**Displacement** 760 tons **Dimensions** 47m x 11m x 4m **Speed** 13 knots **Complement** 22

**Notes**
Minor differences exist between the last ship of the class and the others. Employed in harbour, coastal towage and target towing duties. All the coastal/ocean going tugs have "bolt on" facilities for spraying oil spillages. AGILE is at Gibraltar.

RMAS Capable

## HARBOUR TUGS
## TWIN UNIT TRACTOR TUGS (TUTT'S) CLASS

| Ship | Pennant Number | Completion Date | Builder |
|---|---|---|---|
| FORCEFUL | A221 | 1985 | R. Dunston |
| NIMBLE | A222 | 1985 | R. Dunston |
| POWERFUL | A223 | 1985 | R. Dunston |
| ADEPT | A224 | 1980 | R. Dunston |
| BUSTLER | A225 | 1981 | R. Dunston |
| CAPABLE | A226 | 1981 | R. Dunston |
| CAREFUL | A227 | 1982 | R. Dunston |
| FAITHFUL | A228 | | R. Dunston |
| DEXTEROUS | A231 | | R. Dunston |

**G.R.T.** 375 tons **Dimensions** 39m x 10m x 4m **Speed** 12 knots **Complement** 10

**Notes**
The five new ships of this class will be delivered from mid 1985 onwards to replace the CONFIANCE Class. These vessels have not been entirely suitable for overnight coastal work, due to excessive vibration and noise in accommodation spaces.

RMAS Corgi

## DOG CLASS

| Ship | Penn. No. | Ship | Penn. No. |
|---|---|---|---|
| ALSATIAN | A106 | POINTER | A188 |
| CAIRN | A126 | SETTER | A189 |
| DALMATIAN | A129 | SEALYHAM | A197 |
| DEERHOUND | A155 | SPANIEL | A201 |
| ELKHOUND | A162 | SHEEPDOG | A250 |
| LABRADOR | A168 | FOXHOUND | A326 |
| HUSKY | A178 | BASSET | A327 |
| MASTIFF | A180 | COLLIE | A328 |
| SALUKI | A182 | CORGIE | A330 |

**G.R.T.** 152 tons **Dimensions** 29m x 8m x 4m **Speed** 12 knots **Complement** 8

**Notes**
General harbour tugs — all completed between 1962 & 1972.

RMAS Doris

## IMPROVED GIRL CLASS

| Ship | Penn. No. | Ship | Penn. No. |
|---|---|---|---|
| DAISY | A145 | CHARLOTTE | A210 |
| DAPHNE | A156 | CHRISTINE | A217 |
| DOROTHY | A173 | CLARE | A218 |
| EDITH | A177 | DORIS | A252 |

**G.R.T.** 75 tons **Speed** 10 knots **Complement** 4

**Notes**
All completed 1971-2. CLARE is serving in RN colours and with an RN crew in Hong Kong.

RMAS Lilah

## IRENE CLASS

| Ship | Penn. No. | Ship | Penn. No. |
|---|---|---|---|
| KATHLEEN | A166 | ISABEL | A183 |
| KITTY | A170 | JOAN | A190 |
| LESLEY | A172 | JOYCE | A193 |
| LILAH | A174 | MYRTLE | A199 |
| MARY | A175 | NANCY | A202 |
| IRENE | A181 | NORAH | A205 |

**G.R.T.** 89 tons **Speed** 8 knots **Complement** 4

**Notes**
Known as Water Tractors these craft are used for basin moves and towage of light barges.

RMAS Gwendoline

## FELICITY CLASS

| Ship | Penn. No. | Ship | Penn. No. |
|---|---|---|---|
| FELICITY | A112 | GENEVIEVE | A150 |
| FRANCES | A147 | GEORGINA | A152 |
| FIONA | A148 | GWENDOLINE | A196 |
| FLORENCE | A149 | HELEN | A198 |

**G.R.T.** 80 tons **Speed** 10 knots **Complement** 4

**Notes**
Water Tractors — completed in 1973; FRANCES, FLORENCE & GENEVIEVE completed 1980.

RMAS Whitehead

## TRIALS SHIPS

| Ship | Pennant Number | Completion Date | Builder |
|---|---|---|---|
| WHITEHEAD | A364 | 1971 | Scotts |

**G.R.T.** 3,427 tons **Dimensions** 97m x 15m x 5m **Speed** 15.5 knots **Complement** 50

**Notes**
Fitted with Torpedo Tubes for trial firings.

**RMAS Newton**

| Ship | Pennant Number | Completion Date | Builder |
|---|---|---|---|
| NEWTON | A367 | 1976 | Scotts |

**G.R.T.** 2,779 tons **Dimensions** 99m x 16m x 6m **Speed** 15 knots **Complement** 52

**Notes**
Built as sonar propagation trials ship but can also be used as a Cable Layer.

RMAS Auricula

## TEST & EXPERIMENTAL SONAR TENDER

| Ship | Pennant Number | Completion Date | Builder |
|---|---|---|---|
| AURICULA | A285 | 1981 | Ferguson Bros |

**G.R.T.** 981 tons **Dimensions** 52m x 11m x 3m **Speed** 12 knots **Complement** 22

**Notes**
Employed on evaluation work of new sonar equipment that may equip RN ships of the future.

RMAS Throsk

## ARMAMENT STORES CARRIERS

| Ship | Pennant Number | Completion Date | Builder |
|---|---|---|---|
| KINTERBURY | A378 | 1980 | Appledore SB |
| THROSK | A379 | 1977 | Cleland SB Co. |

**G.R.T.** 1,357 tons **Dimensions** 64m x 12m x 5m **Speed** 14 knots **Complement** 24

**Notes**
2 holds carry Naval armament stores, ammunition and guided missiles. Employed on short coastal journeys between Naval Bases. KINTERBURY varies slightly from earlier sister ship. The Army's Armament Stores Carrier ST GEORGE (A382) is similar.

RMAS Bee

## INSECT CLASS

| Ship | Pennant Number | Completion Date | Builder |
|---|---|---|---|
| BEE | A216 | 1970 | C.D. Holmes |
| CRICKET | A229 | 1972 | Beverley |
| COCKCHAFER | A230 | 1971 | Beverley |
| GNAT | A239 | 1972 | Beverley |
| LADYBIRD | A253 | 1973 | Beverley |
| CICALA | A263 | 1971 | Beverley |
| SCARAB | A272 | 1973 | Beverley |

**G.R.T.** 279 tons **Dimensions** 34m x 8m x 3m **Speed** 10.5 knots **Complement** 7-13

**Notes**
SCARAB is fitted as a Mooring Vessel and COCKCHAFER as a Stores Carrier — remainder are Naval Armament carriers.

RNXS Loyal Volunteer

## LOYAL CLASS

| Ship | Penn. No. | Ship | Penn. No. |
|---|---|---|---|
| LOYAL HELPER | A157 | LOYAL MEDIATOR | A161 |
| SUPPORTER | A158 | LOYAL MODERATOR | A220 |
| LOYAL WATCHER | A159 | LOYAL CHANCELLOR | A1770 |
| LOYAL VOLUNTEER | A160 | LOYAL PROCTOR | A1771 |

**G.R.T.** 112 tons **Dimensions** 24m x 6m x 3m **Speed** 10.5 knots **Complement** 24

**Notes**
All these craft are operated by the Royal Naval Auxiliary Service (RNXS) — men (and women) — who in time of emergency would man these craft for duties as port control vessels. HMS ALERT and VIGILANT are similar and were taken over from the RNXS.

RMAS Dornoch

## (TYPE A, B & X) TENDERS

| Ship | Penn. No. | Ship | Penn. No. |
|---|---|---|---|
| MELTON | A83 | CLOVELLY | A389 |
| MENAI | A84 | CRICCIETH | A391 |
| MEON | A87 | GLENCOE | A392 |
| MILFORD | A91 | DUNSTER | A393 |
| LLANDOVERY | A207 | FINTRY | A394 |
| LAMLASH | A208 | GRASMERE | A402 |
| LECHLADE | A211 | CROMARTY | A488 |
| ILCHESTER* | A308 | DORNOCH | A490 |
| INSTOW* | A309 | HEADCORN | A1766 |
| FOTHERBY | A341 | HEVER | A1767 |
| FELSTEAD | A348 | HARLECH | A1768 |
| ELKSTONE | A353 | HAMBLEDON | A1769 |
| FROXFIELD | A354 | HOLMWOOD | A1772 |
| EPWORTH | A355 | HORNING | A1773 |
| DENMEAD | A363 | | |
| FULBECK | A365 | | |
| CRICKLADE | A381 | DATCHET | A357 |

**G.R.T.** 78 tons **Dimensions** 24m x 6m x 3m **Speed** 10.5 knots **Complement** 5

**Notes**
All completed since 1971 to replace Motor Fishing Vessels. Vessels marked* are diving tenders. Remainder are Training Tenders, Passenger Ferries, or Cargo Vessels. DATCHET (A357) is a diving tender — not of this class but similar — based at Devonport with an RN crew.

RMAS Alnmouth

## ABERDOVEY CLASS ('63 DESIGN)

| Ship | Penn. No. | Ship | Penn. No. |
|---|---|---|---|
| ABERDOVEY | Y10 | BEDDGELERT | A100 |
| ABINGER | Y11 | BEMBRIDGE | A101 |
| ALNESS§ | Y12 | BIBURY | A103 |
| ALNMOUTH | Y13 | BLAKENEY ● | A104 |
| ASHCOTT§ | Y16 | BRODICK | A105 |
| APPLEBY | A383 | CARTMEL | A350 |
| BEAULIEU ● | A99 | CAWSAND | A351 |

**G.R.T.** 77 tons **Dimensions** 24m x 5m x 3m **Speed** 10.5 knots **Complement** 5

**Notes**
ALNMOUTH is a Sea Cadet Training Ship based at Plymouth. ABERDOVEY & BEMBRIDGE have similar duties at Portsmouth. ABINGER administered by RNR (CinC NavHome).
● In service as Harbour tenders at Port Stanley with RN crews.
§ In service at Gibraltar with RN crews.

RNXS Shipham

## INSHORE CRAFT

| Ship | Penn. No. | Ship | Penn. No. |
|---|---|---|---|
| SHIPHAM ● | M2726 | SANDRINGHAM | M2791 |
| PORTISHAM ● | M2781 | | |

**Displacement** 164 tons **Dimensions** 32m x 6m x 2m **Speed** 12 knots **Complement** 24

**Notes**
All are ex Inshore Minesweepers converted for alternative roles. Vessels marked ● are training ships for the RNXS but will be taken out of service when new 20 metre craft are delivered. SANDRINGHAM is used as a Clyde ferry for service personnel but her future is under review.

RMAS Oilstone

## OILPRESS CLASS

| Ship | Pennant Number | Completion Date | Builder |
|---|---|---|---|
| OILPRESS | Y21 | 1969 | Appledore Shipbuilders |
| OILSTONE | Y22 | 1969 | " " |
| OILWELL | Y23 | 1969 | " " |
| OILFIELD | Y24 | 1969 | " " |
| OILBIRD | Y25 | 1969 | " " |
| OILMAN | Y26 | 1969 | " " |

**G.R.T.** 362 tons **Dimensions** 41m x 9m x 3m **Speed** 11 knots **Complement** 8

**Notes**
Employed as Harbour and Coastal Oilers.

RMAS Watershed

## WATER CARRIERS
## WATER CLASS

| Ship | Pennant Number | Completion Date | Builder |
|---|---|---|---|
| WATERFALL | Y17 | 1967 | Drypool Eng Co |
| WATERSHED | Y18 | 1967 | Drypool Eng Co |
| WATERSPOUT | Y19 | 1967 | Drypool Eng Co |
| WATERSIDE | Y20 | 1968 | Drypool Eng Co |
| WATERCOURSE | Y30 | 1974 | Drypool Eng Co |
| WATERFOWL | Y31 | 1974 | Drypool Eng Co |
| WATERMAN | A146 | 1978 | R. Dunston |

**G.R.T.** 263 tons **Dimensions** 40m x 8m x 2m **Speed** 11 knots **Complement** 8

**Notes**
Capable of coastal passages, these craft normally supply either demineralised or fresh water to the Fleet within port limits.

**RMAS Lodestone**

## DEGAUSSING VESSELS
## MAGNET CLASS

| Ship | Pennant Number | Completion Date | Builder |
|---|---|---|---|
| MAGNET | A114 | 1979 | Cleland |
| LODESTONE | A115 | 1980 | Cleland |

**G.R.T.** 828 tons **Dimensions** 55m x 12m x 4m **Speed** 14 knots **Complement** 10

**Notes**
LODESTONE is in Reserve at Portsmouth but available for service at 7 days' notice.

RMAS Torrid

## TORPEDO RECOVERY VESSELS (TRV'S)
## TORRID CLASS

| Ship | Pennant Number | Completion Date | Builder |
|---|---|---|---|
| TORRENT | A127 | 1971 | Cleland SB Co |
| TORRID | A128 | 1972 | Cleland SB Co |

**G.R.T.** 550 tons **Dimensions** 46m x 9m x 3m **Speed** 12 knots **Complement** 18

**Notes**
A stern ramp is built for the recovery of torpedoes fired for trials and exercises. A total of 32 can be carried.

RMAS Toreador

## TORNADO CLASS

| Ship | Pennant Number | Completion Date | Builder |
|---|---|---|---|
| TORNADO | A140 | 1979 | Hall Russell |
| TORCH | A141 | 1980 | Hall Russell |
| TORMENTOR | A142 | 1980 | Hall Russell |
| TOREADOR | A143 | 1980 | Hall Russell |

**G.R.T.** 560 tons **Dimensions** 47m x 8m x 3m **Speed** 14 knots **Complement** 14

RMAS Pintail

## WILD DUCK CLASS

| Ship | Pennant Number | Completion Date | Builder |
|---|---|---|---|
| MANDARIN | P192 | 1964 | C. Laird |
| PINTAIL | P193 | 1964 | C. Laird |
| GARGANEY | P194 | 1966 | Brooke Marine |
| GOLDENEYE | P195 | 1966 | Brooke Marine |
| GOOSANDER | A164 | 1973 | Robb Caledon |
| POCHARD | A165 | 1973 | Robb Caledon |

**G.R.T.** 900 tons* **Dimensions** 58mm x 12m x 4m **Speed** 10 knots
**Complement** 23-26
* Vessels vary slightly

**Notes**
Vessels capable of carrying out a wide range of duties laying moorings and heavy lift salvage work. 50 tons can be lifted over the horns and 200 tons over the bow.

RMAS Kinloss

## KIN CLASS

| Ship | Pennant Number | Completion Date | Builder |
|---|---|---|---|
| KINGARTH | A232 | 1945 | A Hall Aberdeen |
| KINBRACE | A281 | 1944 | A. Hall Aberdeen |
| KINLOSS | A482 | 1945 | A. Hall Aberdeen |
| UPLIFTER ● | A507 | 1944 | Smith's Dock |

**Displacement** 1,050 tons **Dimensions** 54m x 11m x 4m **Speed** 9 knots **Complement** 23-26

**Notes**

Coastal Salvage Vessels re-engined between 1963 & 1967. Now have same role as Wild Duck Class. SALMASTER, SALMOOR & SALMAID will replace these 40 year old vessels when completed.
● To Reserve mid 1985.

RMAS Dolwen

## DOLWEN CLASS

| Ship | Pennant Number | Completion Date | Builder |
|---|---|---|---|
| DOLWEN (ex Hector Gulf) | A362 | 1962 | P.K. Harris |

**Displacement** 602 tons **Dimensions** 41m x 9m x 4m **Speed** 14 knots **Complement** 12

**Notes**
Built as a stern trawler, then purchased for use as a Buoy tender — now used as Safety Vessel for RAE ABERPORTH (S. Wales) from her base at Pembroke Dock. ENDEAVOUR is a Torpedo Recovery/Trials Vessel at Portland.

# ARMY VESSELS

HMAV Ardennes

## ARMY LANDING CRAFT

**LCL CLASS** | **LANDING CRAFT LOGISTIC**

| Vessel | Pennant Number | Completion Date | Builder |
|---|---|---|---|
| HMAV Ardennes | L4001 | 1977 | Brooke Marine |
| HMAV Arakan | L4002 | 1978 | Brooke Marine |

**Displacement** 1,050 tons **Dimensions** 72m x 15m x 2m **Speed** 10 knots **Complement** 35

**Notes**
Designed to carry up to 350 tons — up to Five Chieftain tanks — loaded onto open beaches through bow doors. Both are mainly used for missile transportation to the Royal Artillery ranges in the Outer Hebrides.

HMAV Andalsnes

**RCL CLASS** **RAMPED CRAFT LOGISTIC**

| Vessel | Pennant Number | Completion Date | Builder |
|---|---|---|---|
| RCTV Arromanches | L105 | 1981 | Brooke Marine |
| RCTV Antwerp | L106 | 1981 | Brooke Marine |
| RCTV Andalsnes | L107 | 1984 | James & Stone |
| RCTV Abbeville | L108 | 1985 | James & Stone |
| RCTV Akyab | L109 | 1985 | James & Stone |

**Displacement** 165 tons **Dimensions** 30m x 8m x 2m **Speed** 9 knots **Complement** 6

**Notes**
Smaller—"all purpose" landing craft capable of carrying up to 100 tons. In service in coastal waters around Cyprus, Hong Kong & UK.

# AIRCRAFT OF THE FLEET AIR ARM

**British Aerospace V-STOL Sea Harrier FRS 1**

The Sea Harrier is a maritime strike/fighter/reconnaissance aircraft now in service operating from the carriers, HMS Invincible and Illustrious. 24 aircraft are in service or reserve. A further 14 are on order — for delivery in 1985. Can carry a variety of weapons which include: sidewinder missiles, 2″ rocket pods, bombs and 30mm Aden guns. The aircraft will eventually carry the Sea Eagle missile.

**Scottish Aviation Jetstream**

The 'flying classroom' for Fleet Air Arm Observers, based at RNAS Culdrose, Cornwall. 16 in service & 4 Mk3 Aircraft on order **Crew** 1/2 (Plus instructor and two student observers) **Length** 48′ **Height** 18′ **Wing Span** 52′ **Speed** 215 knots.

**Westland SEA KING Mk2**

Anti-submarine helicopter fitted with advance avionics including dipping sonar and radar. Armed with torpedoes and depth charges. Able to operate in all weathers and at night. Can also be used for long range Search & Rescue missions. **Crew** Four **Length** 72′ **Height** 17′ **Rotor Diameter** 62′ **Speed** 125 knots. All Mk2 aircraft will eventually be upgraded to Mk5 standards.

**Westland SEA KING Mk4 COMMANDO**

A close derivative of the ASW Sea King. Non retractable under-carriage. Able to lift underslung loads of 8,000 lbs. Can carry 27 fully equipped Royal Marines. 21 aircraft will be in service by the end of 1985. **Crew** Three **Length** 56′ **Height** 16′ **Rotor Diameter** 62′ **Speed** 140 knots.
Powered by two Rolls Royce Gnome (uprated) engines.

**Westland SEA KING Mk5**

An updated version of the Sea King Mk2. A more sophisticated electronic package and new radome have been installed. A Mark 6 aircraft is being developed for service in 1986/7.

**SEA KING AEW**

A modified version of the Sea King Mk2. As a result of the Falklands conflict 2 aircraft were fitted with an advanced airborne early warning radar which is housed in the retractable bulbous dome. Particulars as for Sea King Mk2. Up to 8 aircraft will be delivered during 1985/6—all for service in 849 Squadron.

**Westland WASP**

Anti-submarine and FPB helicopter carried by older frigates. Armed with 2 torpedoes or missiles. Also carried for general duties in H Class Survey Ships. Being replaced by the Lynx. 27 are in service but the majority will be phased out by 1987. A few remaining after this date for service in survey ships. **Crew** 1/2 **Length** 40′ **Height** 11′ **Rotor Diameter** 32′ **Speed** 110 knots. Powered by one Rolls Royce Nimbus turboshaft engine.

**Westland LYNX**

Anti-submarine attack, surface search and strike helicopter. Replacing the Wasp in small ships of the fleet. 56 Mk2 versions & 20 Mk3 versions now in service. Can be armed with 2 homing torpedoes, depth charges or missiles. **Crew** Two **Length** 49′ **Height** 11′ **Rotor Diameter** 42′ **Speed** 150 knots. 3 Mk3 aircraft are on ordor. Power by two Rolls Royce Gem turboshaft engines.

**Westland WESSEX Mk 5**

Utility helicopter used primarily as a troop and stores carrier in support of Royal Marine Commandos. Also used in SAR Role at Culdrose, Portland and Lee-on-Solent. **Crew** 1/2 pilots + aircrew-man. Built in large numbers but now only 24 in service. Only 16 will remain, for secondary duties, after 1986. **Length** 65′ **Height** 16′ **Rotor Diameter** 65′ **Speed** 115 knots.
Powered by two Rolls Royce Bristol Gnome engines.

**Westland/Aerospatiale GAZELLE**

Basic Helicopter Trainer for the Royal Navy and used operationally by the Royal Marines. 19 in service with the Fleet Air Arm at RNAS Culdrose. **Crew** One **Length** 39′ **Height** 10′ **Rotor Diameter** 34′ **Speed** 164 knots.
Power by one Turbo meca Astazou 111A turboshaft engine.

---

## ADDITIONAL AIRCRAFT

In addition to the aircraft illustrated the following aircraft have Naval functions.

CANBERRA's of 360 Sqdn. A joint RN/RAF Electronic Countermeasures Squadron based at RAF Wyton.

A further 12 CANBERRAS & 23 HUNTERS are based at RNAS Yeovilton and are flown & maintained by civilian contractors. They have a variety of Fleet Requirement tasks (Target towing etc) & general flying duties for the Air Direction school.

10 CHIPMUNK aircraft operate the Flying Grading Flight at Plymouth Airport for officers under training at Dartmouth. Civilian maintained.

2 HS125 aircraft are owned by the RN and operate as part of 32 Sqdn RAF (VIP Communications) at RAF Northolt.

The Historic Flight of the Fleet Air Arm (Seahawk, Swordfish, Sea Fury, Firefly, Tiger Moth & Harvard) are based at Yeovilton.

## Communications Aircraft

RNAS Yeovilton operate 4 Sea Herons and RNAS Culdrose operate 2 Sea Devons for Fishery Protection and General Communications Duties.

### Sea Heron C Mk 1 (top)

**Crew** 2/3 **Length** 48′ **Height** 16′ **Wing Span** 71′ **Speed** 182 knots.. Powered by 4 Gypsy Queen Air Cooled engines.

### Sea Devon C Mk 20 (bottom)

**Crew** 2 **Length** 39′ **Height** 13′ **Wing Span** 57′ **Speed** 205 knots. Powered by 2 Gypsy Queen Air Cooled engines.

# At the end of the line . . .

Readers may well find other warships afloat which are not mentioned in this book. The majority have fulfilled a long and useful life and are now relegated to non-seagoing duties. The following list gives details of their current duties:

| Penn. No. | Ship | Remarks |
|---|---|---|
| A134 | RAME HEAD | Maintenance Ship. Used as an Accommodation Ship at Rosyth |
| A191 | BERRY HEAD | As above, but at Devonport. |
| C35 | BELFAST | World War II Cruiser On permanent display — Pool of London |
| D73 | CAVALIER | World War II Destroyer. Museum Ship at Brighton. (Open to the public). |
| D12 | KENT | County Class Destroyer— Accommodation & Sea Cadet Training Ship at Portsmouth |
| F108 | LONDONDERRY | Type 12 Frigate Harbour Training Ship—Gosport |
| F97<br>F117 | RUSSELL<br>&<br>ASHANTI | Captain & Tribal Class Frigates. Engineers Harbour Training Ships at Gosport |
| S05 | FINWHALE | Porpoise Class Submarine Harbour Training Ship at Gosport |
| S67 | ALLIANCE | Submarine Museum Ship at Gosport (Open to the public) |

**At the time of publishing the following ships were awaiting tow for scrap or sale.**

PORTSMOUTH
Tiger (C20)
Eskimo (F119)
Rhyl (F129)
Nubian (F131)

PLYMOUTH
Forth (A187)
Salisbury (F32)

ROSYTH
Brighton (F106)
Dreadnought (S101)
Lofoten
Tenacity
Thornham (M2793)
Laleston (M1158)
Eastbourne (F73)
Duncan (F80)
Lewiston (M1208)
Stalker